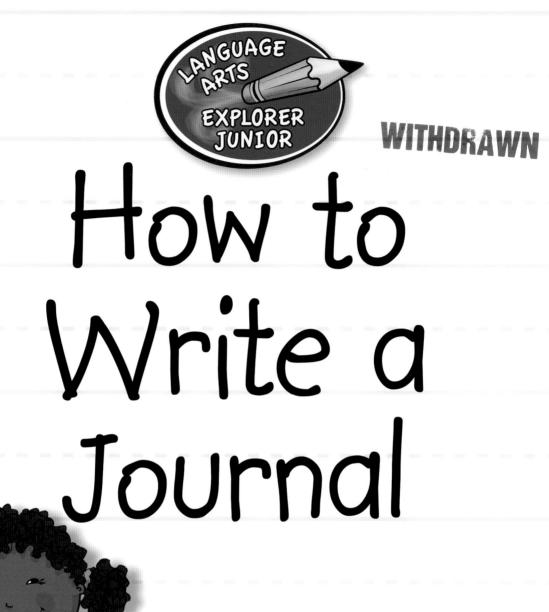

LANGUAGE ARTS

EXPLORER JUNIOR

How to Write a Journal

by Cecilia Minden
and Kate Roth

MICHIGAN

Published in the United States of America by Cherry Lake Publishing
Ann Arbor, Michigan
www.cherrylakepublishing.com

Content Adviser: Jeannette Mancilla-Martinez, EdD, Assistant Professor of
Literacy, Language, and Culture, University of Illinois at Chicago

Design and Illustration: The Design Lab

Photo Credits: Page 4, ©iStockphoto.com/Maica; page 6, ©iStockphoto.
com/flashon; page 11, ©iStockphoto.com/DIGIcal; page 21,
©iStockphoto.com/gbh007

Library of Congress Cataloging-in-Publication Data
Minden, Cecilia.
  How to write a journal/by Cecilia Minden and Kate Roth.
     p. cm.–(Language arts explorer junior)
  Includes bibliographical references and index.
  ISBN-13: 978-1-60279-994-3 (lib. bdg.)
  ISBN-10: 1-60279-994-6 (lib. bdg.)
  1. Diaries–Authorship–Juvenile literature. I. Roth, Kate. II. Title.
  PN4390.M56 2011
  808'.06692–dc22   2010031317

Cherry Lake Publishing would like to acknowledge the work
of The Partnership for 21st Century Skills. Please visit
www.21stcenturyskills.org for more information.

Printed in the United States of America
Corporate Graphics Inc.
January 2011
CLSP08

Table of Contents

CHAPTER ONE

All About You

You can take your journal anywhere you go.

A **journal** is a written collection of your feelings and thoughts. It is a place where you can record your **opinions**. You can also write about events. What you write about is up to you!

You can keep a journal in different ways. Some people type their journals using computers. Others handwrite in notebooks. Here's what you'll need to complete the activities in this book:

- Notebook
- Pen

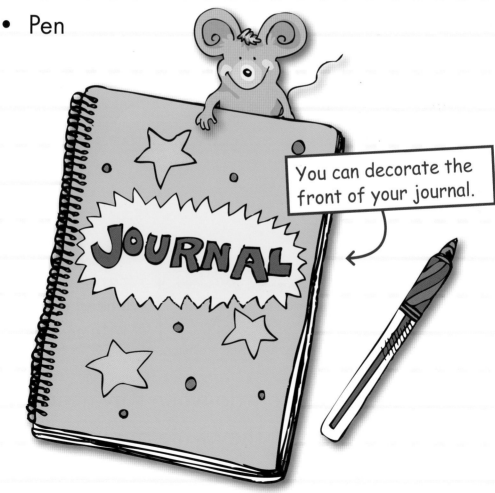

You can decorate the front of your journal.

Write About a Place

What do you do when you need to come up with an idea?

What do many writers do when they need an idea to write about? They write about what they know.

For your first journal **entry**, write about a place. To get started, think about a place you know well. Close your eyes. Picture that place in your head. In your journal, you can describe the place. You can also write about why it is important to you.

Think of some of your favorite places to go.

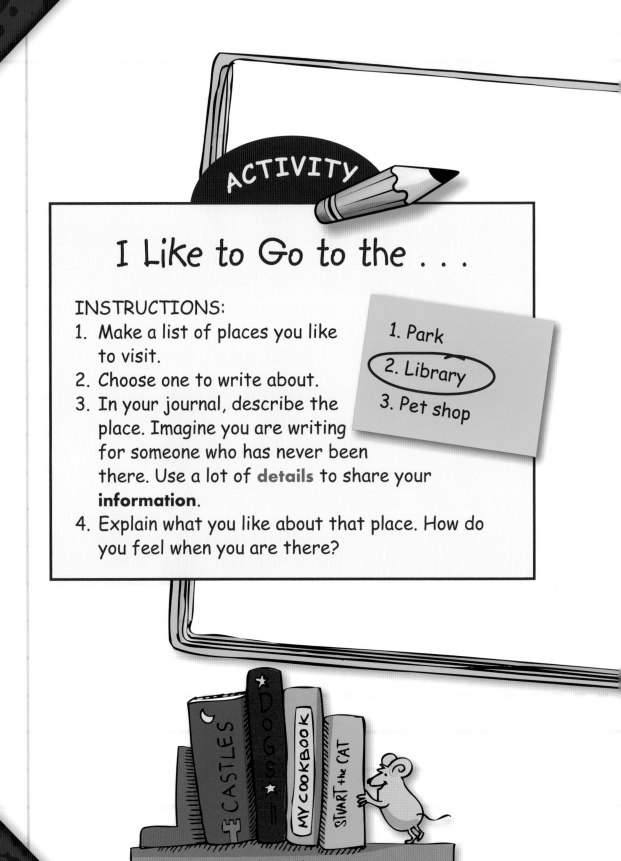

ACTIVITY

I Like to Go to the . . .

INSTRUCTIONS:
1. Make a list of places you like to visit.
2. Choose one to write about.
3. In your journal, describe the place. Imagine you are writing for someone who has never been there. Use a lot of **details** to share your **information**.
4. Explain what you like about that place. How do you feel when you are there?

1. Park
2. Library
3. Pet shop

August 15, 2012

I like to go to the library in the summer. It is hot outside. The library is nice and cool. There are so many books! I like the smell of library books. You have to be quiet in the library because people are reading. I don't mind being quiet. I feel calm at the library. I check out a stack of books every time I go there. I wonder who read the books before me.

CHAPTER THREE

Write About an Event

Maybe going to the movies is one of your favorite events.

Do you need another idea? Write about an event. An event is something that happens. Events are usually special in some way.

Try writing about an exciting day.

Use your senses to describe the event. What did you see? What did you hear? What could you smell? Did you feel happy or scared?

Make a short list before you write the journal entry. Put the action of the event in the order in which it happened. This is called **chronological** order.

ACTIVITY

Guess What Happened?

INSTRUCTIONS:
1. Think of events that happened to you.
2. Choose one to write about.
3. Try to remember everything that happened.
4. List what happened in chronological order.
5. Use the list to help you write your journal entry.

1. Dad and I went to the movies.
2. He lost his wallet.
3. We could not buy tickets.
4. I found the wallet.
5. We saw a movie.

TICKET

September 2, 2012

Dad took me to the movies yesterday. We went to buy tickets. I could smell fresh popcorn. Dad reached in his pocket. His wallet was gone! We headed back to the car. That was when I saw something by one of the tires. "Look, Dad! Is that your wallet?" I asked.

Dad smiled. It was his wallet. I was so happy. We got lucky that day! I asked Dad what we would do if we ever found someone's wallet. He said we would take it to a police station.

Dad paid for the movies. I got a treat for saving the day. It was a big bucket of popcorn. Yum!

CHAPTER FOUR

Write About Your Feelings

A journal is just for you. Writing can help you think about feelings. What makes you sad? What makes you happy? Writing can help you understand your feelings.

ACTIVITY

Have You Ever Felt . . . .

INSTRUCTIONS:
1. Choose a feeling.
2. Think about things that make you feel that way.
3. Write about the feeling you chose in your journal.

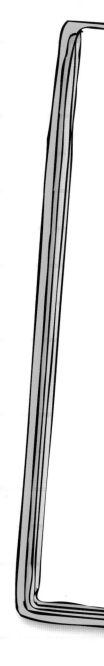

Things that make
me feel scared:
1. Thunderstorms
2. High places
3. Spiders

September 24, 2012

I am scared of spiders. They are creepy looking. If I think about them crawling on me, I start to shake. My teacher says spiders are an important part of nature. I'm not so sure. Some spiders can jump. Those are the worst. I know I'm a lot bigger than spiders. I'm still afraid of them!

CHAPTER FIVE

Write About Your Opinion

A journal is a great place to write your opinions. You can write about why you like or do not like something. Maybe you are not sure how you feel. That's okay. Try putting both sides of the story on paper. This can help you sort out your thoughts.

ACTIVITY

What Do You Think?

INSTRUCTIONS:
1. Make a list of three things you do not like.
2. Choose one to write about.
3. Write about what you don't like in your journal.
4. Be sure to explain your opinion.

Things I Don't Like:
1. Wet socks
2. Bedtime
3. Peas

October 1, 2012

I do not like to eat peas! They are wrinkled green balls that fall off my fork. I can't stand how they squish in my mouth. I think they taste slimy.

My parents like peas. That means I have to eat them. Mom says I need to eat my vegetables. In my opinion, cake should count as a vegetable!

CHAPTER SIX

Write About Your Wishes and Dreams

Do you have any wishes or dreams? Do you ever wish you could do something special? What do you dream of doing when you get older? Write about these wishes and dreams in your journal.

ACTIVITY

What Did You Wish For?

1. Make a list of your wishes or dreams.
2. Choose one to write about.
3. Write about it in your journal.

THINGS I'M WISHING FOR
1. Getting a puppy
2. Having a sleep-over with my friend
3. Riding a skateboard

October 8, 2012

I wish I knew how to ride a skateboard. I would make up great tricks and teach them to my friends. We would put on skateboarding shows. The crowd would cheer. I would be a skateboarding star.

CHAPTER SEVEN

Keep Writing!

What treasures can be found in your journal?

You are a special person with many things to say. Journals are books full of your thoughts and feelings. Keep writing! Keep your journals in a safe place. You may want to read them again years from now. How might you change as you get older? Will you have the same interests or the same worries? It will be fun to look back on your life as a kid!

You can share writing ideas with your friends.

Glossary

chronological (kron-uh-LOJ-uh-kuhl) arranged in the order in which things happened

details (DEE-taylz) separate bits of information about something

entry (EN-tree) a piece of information in a journal

information (in-fur-MAY-shuhn) knowledge and facts

journal (JUR-nuhl) a record of one's thoughts and ideas

opinions (uh-PIN-yuhnz) a person's beliefs and ideas about somebody or something

For More Information

BOOKS

Becker,Suzy. *Kids Make It Better: A Write-In, Draw-In Journal.*
New York: Workman Publishing Company, 2010.

Loewen, Nancy. *It's All About You: Writing Your Own Journal.*
Minneapolis: Picture Window Books, 2009.

WEB SITES

Activity TV—Origami: Journal
www.activitytv.com/812-journal
Look here to learn how to make a simple journal.

KidsHealth—What to Do if You Can't Sleep
kidshealth.org/kid/stay_healthy/body/cant_sleep.html
Find out how writing in a journal can help you catch some z's.

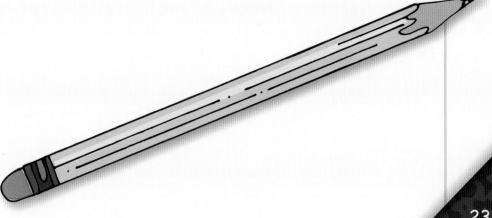

Index

About the Authors

Cecilia Minden, PhD, is the former Director of the Language and Literacy Program at Harvard Graduate School of Education. While at Harvard, Dr. Minden taught several writing courses for teachers. She is now a full-time literacy consultant and the author of more than 100 books for children. Dr. Minden lives in Chapel Hill, North Carolina, with her husband, Dave Cupp, and a cute but spoiled Yorkie named Kenzie.

Kate Roth has a doctorate from Harvard University in Language and Literacy and a masters from Columbia University Teachers College in Curriculum and Teaching. Her work focuses on writing instruction in the primary grades. She has taught first grade, kindergarten, and Reading Recovery. She has also instructed hundreds of teachers from around the world in early literacy practices. She lives in Shanghai, China, with her husband and three children, ages 2, 6, and 9. They do a lot of writing to stay in touch with friends and family and record their experiences.